Animal Classification

Fish

Angela Royston

raintree

Raintree is an imprint of Capstone Global Library Limited, a company incorporated in England and Wales having its registered office at 7 Pilgrim Street, London, EC4V 6LB – Registered company number: 6695582

www.raintree.co.uk
myorders@raintree.co.uk

Edited by Helen Cox Cannons, Clare Lewis and Abby Colich
Designed by Steve Mead
Picture research by Tracy Cummins
Production by Victoria Fitzgerald
Originated by Capstone Global Library Ltd
Printed and bound in China

ISBN 978 1 406 28738 7 (hardback)
18 17 16 15 14
10 9 8 7 6 5 4 3 2 1

ISBN 978 1 406 28745 5 (paperback)
19 18 17 16
10 9 8 7 6 5 4 3 2 1

British Library Cataloguing in Publication Data
A full catalogue record for this book is available from the British Library.

reproduce photographs: FLPA: Minden, 15, 29 Middle; Getty Images: R.Duran, 9; Science Photo Library: Lawrence Naylor, 24; Shutterstock: Beth Swanson, 7, David Byron Keener, 4, Dray van Beeck, 5, Evok20, 6, feathercollector, 14, Imageman, Design Element, Joe Belanger, 19, Krzysztof Odziomek, 11, Mariusz Niedzwiedzki, 22, 29 Top, Mircea BEZERGHEANU, Cover, Roman Vintonyak, 8, Sekundator, 25, Steffi Sawyer, 18, Vlad61, 16, 17, Wiratchai wansamngam, 12; SuperStock: Animals Animals, 20, Biosphoto, 21, Mark Conlin, 13, Minden Pictures, 26, NaturePL, 23, 27, 29 Bottom; Thinkstock: Sylwia Domaradzka, 10, 28.

We would like to thank Michael Bright for his invaluable help in the preparation of this book.

Every effort has been made to contact copyright holders of material reproduced in this book. Any omissions will be rectified in subsequent printings if notice is given to the publisher.

Acknowledgements
We would like to thank the following for permission to

Contents

Some words are shown in bold, **like this**. You can find out what they mean by looking in the glossary.

Meet the fish

Salmon, angelfish and sharks are three different types of fish. There are thousands of other types of fish. Some live in **fresh water,** but most fish live in the sea.

Colourful angelfish live on coral reefs in the sea.

A blue shark is one of the fastest sharks.

Scientists sort living things into groups. This is called **classification**. The animals in each group have certain things in common. Fish live in water, breathe through **gills** and have **fins**.

Body shape

Fish belong to a larger group of animals called **vertebrates**. Birds and reptiles are also vertebrates. A vertebrate has a hard **skeleton** inside its body. Different parts of the skeleton form a head, backbone and usually a tail, too.

Most fish swim by moving their tails from side to side.

A flat fish swims by moving its tail up and down because it swims on its side.

Many fish have a smooth shape with a pointed head, which allows them to move easily through the water. Fish that live on the seabed are often round and flat.

Groups of fish

Scientists divide fish into three groups. The biggest group is the bony fish, such as trout and sole. They have **fins** and their **skeletons** are made of bones.

A stingray is wide and flat, with **venomous** stingers in its tail.

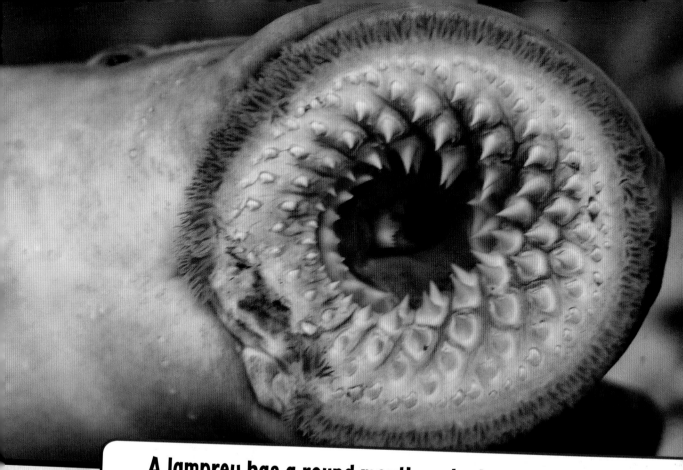

A lamprey has a round mouth and a long, thin body.

Sharks and rays form a separate group. They have fins but their skeletons are made of a rubbery substance called **cartilage**. The smallest group is the jawless fish, such as lampreys. They have no jaws and no side fins.

Sharks

Sharks are among the fiercest fish. Most sharks have many sharp teeth and some can swim fast. They use their amazing sense of smell to detect faint **scents** of **prey** several kilometres away.

A great white shark is one of the most dangerous sharks to humans.

The biggest whale shark ever found was over 12 metres (41 feet) long.

A whale shark is the largest shark, and the largest fish. Although it is so big, it is not fierce at all. It feeds on zooplankton (very tiny animals).

Fins

Fish have **fins** on their tail, their sides, their belly and their back. They use the tail fin to move forwards and the fins on their sides to steer and to slow down.

You can see the different types of fins on this colourful fish.

dorsal fin

pectoral fin

tail fin

pelvic fin

A shark's fin cutting through the sea warns people that a shark is near.

The fin on a fish's back stops it from rolling over in the water. A shark has a large fin on its back, which sometimes breaks through the surface of the water as it swims.

Flying fish

Flying fish can jump out of the water and glide through the air! They have extra large side **fins,** which they use like wings. Flying fish swim fast before they leap into the air.

A flying fish can jump over 1.2 metres (4 feet) high into the air.

A flying fish can glide for 400 metres (1,300 feet).

Flying fish use their tail to stay in the air.
As they begin to drop, they push their tail
against the surface of the water to raise
themselves up again.

Colourful fish

Bony fish have hard, see-through **scales**, which stop their skin from being hurt. Some fish have skin with bright spots or stripes, which show through the scales.

A lionfish's bright colours warn other sea animals that it has **venomous** spines and is bad to eat.

A sole is coloured to look just like the seabed it swims over.

The colours of some fish blend in with their surroundings. This is called **camouflage**. It helps them to hide from other sea animals that might want to eat them!

Gills

Almost all living things need to take in the gas oxygen to survive. Land animals breathe air in and out of their lungs. Fish take in oxygen from the water as it passes over their **gills**.

Bony fish have a special flap that covers the gills.

gill slits

gill flap

A shark has several gill slits between its head and its side **fins**.

As water passes over the gills, oxygen moves from the water into the fish's blood. At the same time, carbon dioxide moves out of the fish's blood into the water.

Laying eggs

Many fish begin life inside an egg that floats in the water. The egg may be one of thousands laid by the mother. Many eggs are eaten by other fish. The rest of them **hatch** into fish, which then grow bigger.

Some of these fish eggs are beginning to hatch.

A male stickleback guards its nest of eggs.

Sticklebacks look after their eggs, which makes them different from many other fish. The male stickleback builds a nest and guards the eggs until they have hatched.

Seahorses

A seahorse is unlike any other fish. Its head is shaped like a horse's head and it clings to sea grass and coral with its tail.

Seahorses have small **fins** and move slowly.

Like sticklebacks, seahorses look after their eggs. The male seahorse holds the eggs inside a **pouch** on his body. He keeps them safe until they are ready to **hatch**.

You can just see a young seahorse's tail at the top of its father's pouch.

Shark babies

Sharks produce only a few eggs at a time. Some shark eggs are protected inside their own special case.

A swell shark's egg case is sometimes known as a mermaid's purse.

Young blacktip reef sharks keep together in shallow water until they have grown bigger.

Blacktip reef sharks, tiger sharks and many other sharks do not lay eggs. Instead, the tiny sharks grow inside the mother's body until they are big enough to be born. Then they leave the mother and swim away.

Strange deep-sea fish

Most fish live near the surface of the sea, where there is lots of daylight. Only a few fish live deep in the oceans, where it is always dark. These fish include gulper eels and anglerfish.

A gulper eel has such a huge mouth, it can swallow fish larger than itself.

An anglerfish makes a special light to attract prey.

It is hard for deep-sea fish to find food.
An anglerfish has a special **fin** with a light
at the end. The light attracts **prey** right into
the anglerfish's mouth.

Quiz

Look at the pictures below and read the clues. Can you remember the names of these fish? Look back in the book if you need help.

1. I have lots of sharp teeth and a very good sense of smell. What am I?

Answers

1. shark
2. seahorse
3. flying fish
4. angler fish

2. I keep my babies in a **pouch** until they are ready to **hatch.** What am I?

3. I use my **fins** like wings. What am I?

4. I dangle my light just above my mouth to attract **prey.** What am I?

Glossary

camouflage when an animal blends in with its surroundings

cartilage tough, rubbery material that sharks and rays have instead of bone

classification system that scientists use to divide living things into separate groups

fin bendy flap that sticks out from a fish's body and helps it to move through the water

fresh water water in ponds, lakes, streams and rivers, which is not salty

gills parts of the body that allow fish to take in the gas oxygen from water

hatch break out of an egg

pouch part of the body that is like a pocket in the skin

prey animal that is hunted by another animal for food

scales small, hard plates that cover an animal's skin

scent smell of an animal

skeleton hard, bony frame inside the body. It is the skeleton that gives vertebrate animals their shape.

venomous full of venom. Venom is poison that is injected by a sting or bite.

vertebrate animal that has a backbone and skeleton inside its body

Find out more

Books

Fantastic Fish, Isabel Thomas (Raintree, 2013)

Fish, Squid and Jellyfish (Deadly Factbook), Steve Backshall (Orion Books, 2013)

Why do Fish have Gills?, Pat Jacobs (Franklin Watts, 2014)

Websites

animals.nationalgeographic.com/animals/fish
This section of National Geographic's website includes photos and information about sharks, eels and other fish. Just click on the photos!

www.bbc.co.uk/nature/life/Actinopterygii/by/rank/all
This BBC website has videos of lots of different fish.

Index